MICHAEL'S STORY

Emotional Abuse and Working with a Counselor

by Deborah Anderson
and Martha Finne

Illustrated by Jeanette Swofford

Dillon Press, Inc. Minneapolis, Minnesota 55415

To Flossie Finnicum, social worker; the administration; and, most of all, the children of Jefferson Elementary School

Illustrations courtesy of Hennepin County Medical Society Auxiliary, Inc.

Library of Congress Cataloging in Publication Data

Anderson, Deborah, 1946-
  Michael's story.

  Summary: Reports the case of a boy who was emotionally abused and what happened when he worked with a counselor. Includes sources of help for abused children.
  1. Child abuse—Juvenile literature. 2. Abused children—Counseling of—Juvenile literature. [1. Child abuse]
  I. Finne, Martha. II. Title.
  HV713.A52   1986   362.7'044   85-25400
  ISBN 0-87518-322-0

Dillon Press, Inc., 242 Portland Avenue South
Minneapolis, Minnesota 55415

Printed in the United States of America
    2 3 4 5 6 7 8 9 10 95 94 93 92 91 90 89 88 87

Contents

Michael's Story

Once, Michael Boyd thought that no one liked him. His parents always used to yell at him and tell him he was not smart. He had no friends at school, either. But one year things changed for Michael and his family.

One morning before school, Michael was reading about space travel while his mother fixed his sister's hair. He asked his mother question after question about being an astronaut.

"How good do my grades have to be?" he asked.

"Michael, stop bothering me about this now, okay? I have to get dressed for my exercise class," Mom said. "Go ask your dad."

"But, Mom, why can't I. . ." Michael started to say.

His mother interrupted, "Michael, didn't I tell you that I'm busy?"

Michael went downstairs into the kitchen.

"Michael," said Dad, "how about combing your hair before you eat breakfast? It's a mess."

"Dad," said Michael, "I was wondering. How good do my grades have to be so I can be an astronaut?"

"What does that have to do with combing your hair?" asked Dad.

"Nothing," said Michael, looking at the floor.

"I don't want to sit across the table from a messy kid," said Dad. "Go comb your hair and then I'll talk to you."

Michael went into the bathroom near the kitchen. He combed his hair. Back in the kitchen, he poured his cereal and milk. Dad was reading the newspaper and drinking coffee.

"Dad," said Michael, "I combed my hair."

Dad put down his newspaper. "I see," he said. "Now, what's this about being an astronaut?"

"Well, I was reading about space

travel," Michael said, "and I want to know how to be an astronaut."

Dad said, "How could you ever become an astronaut when you can't even remember to comb your hair? Your mother and I have to nag you all the time to get you to do your chores, too. And when you do work, half the things you do are wrong!" His voice got louder and louder as he talked.

Mother and Ali came into the kitchen.

"Michael! What did you do to make your father so angry?" Mom asked. "Can't we ever have a peaceful breakfast?"

Michael didn't say anything. Whenever his mom and dad sounded angry, he tried to be as quiet as he could be. He just kept eating his cereal.

"He thinks he can be an astronaut," said Dad. "But I doubt it. He's too lazy."

"Oh, George," said Mom. "You're always so hard on him."

"I wouldn't have to be if you saw to it that he did something around here!" Dad shouted.

"You don't have to yell," said Mom.

"I'm going to the office," said Dad. He slammed the door as he left.

"Michael, why do you always have to make him blow up like that?" asked Mom.

"I don't know," Michael said sadly. He didn't understand what he did to make his dad so angry.

Mom and Ali ate breakfast. Then

Mom stood up and said, "I have to go to my class now. Michael, don't forget to take out the garbage. And this time, try to remember to put the cover on. You always leave it off."

She kissed Ali and patted Michael on the head. They heard her car as she drove away.

Michael carried their dishes to the sink. Then he took out the garbage. I'd love to just go float in space, he thought. Then Mom and Dad couldn't yell at me. It would be so quiet there.

Michael came back in. Ali was putting on her coat. Michael ate a cookie and put some in his jacket pocket to eat on the way to school.

"I'm going to tell Mom!" said Ali.

"Better not!" said Michael. "You're such a tattle-tale!"

They locked the back door and walked to school through the fallen leaves. Michael and Ali lived only two blocks from school, so they walked every day.

When they got to school, two boys from Michael's second-grade class ran up to him. "Hey, Fatty, what's in your backpack?" asked one.

"None of your business," said Michael.

"I'll bet it's more candy," said the other as he grabbed it and tried to take it.

"Leave my backpack alone. It's mine!" yelled Michael. Ali ran into the school. Michael hit the boy who grabbed his backpack. He kicked at the other boy but missed him. The second boy tripped

Michael, then hit him. Michael fell
down. It hurt a lot, and tears came to
his eyes.

"Aw, leave the creep alone. We'll get
him at recess," said the first boy. The
two boys ran into the school. Michael
stood outside until he was sure they
were gone.

Slowly Michael walked to his locker.
Why does everyone pick on me? he
wondered. He felt very sad. He looked
sad, too. Michael didn't get along well
with other kids. He didn't have any
friends. During recess he usually sat by
himself and watched the others play.
When the other kids did notice him,
Michael often ended up in fights with
them.

Just then Mr. Mason, the social worker, walked over. "I saw what just happened outside. Looks like you, Scott, and Tom got into another fight," he said. "Let's go to my office for a few minutes and talk about it."

"What about my teacher? I'll be late," said Michael. He was worried.

"It's all right. I just saw her. She thinks it's a good idea for us to talk," said Mr. Mason. Mr. Mason and Michael had talked together once last year and once this year. Both times Michael had had big fights with other kids.

Mr. Mason's office was sort of messy. Michael liked that. At home, everything had to be neat. There were lots of papers and books on the desk, and on the walls were drawings by kids, signs, and posters. Best of all, there was a window overlooking the playground. Mr. Mason looked kind of messy, too. His clothes looked old and comfortable.

"Those two boys seemed to be giving you a hard time," Mr. Mason said.

"Yeah, they always do," said Michael. "Everyone does."

"Everyone does? Even your teacher?" asked Mr. Mason.

"No, I guess Ms. Kline doesn't," said Michael.

"Ms. Kline and I talked about you. She's a little worried. She said your tests are good and you can do good work, but you don't. She also said you often look sad, and sometimes angry."

Michael looked at the floor. He didn't know what to say.

"I care about you, Michael. My job at school is to help kids. I'd like to see you happier here," Mr. Mason said. "Is the problem that you don't like school?"

"No, I like school," Michael said.

"Do you have many friends here?" asked Mr. Mason.

"No," Michael said. He felt sad and angry about that. Michael really didn't think anyone liked him.

"You have a sister at home, don't you?" Mr. Mason asked. "Do you get along with her?"

Boy! Michael thought, he sure asks a lot of questions! But he told Mr. Mason about Ali.

Just then the phone rang. "I have a student here right now," Michael heard him say into the phone. "OK, I'll be right there." Mr. Mason hung up and said to Michael, "I have to go to the office for a few minutes. While I'm gone, why don't you think about what it's like for you at home? We'll talk more when I get back. If you need anything, my aide is in the next room."

Michael sat and looked out of the window. He thought about his dad. Sometimes he liked it when his dad was gone on business trips. Michael thought, I wish Dad liked me as much as he likes Ali. She gets away with everything. Mom likes her better, too.

That reminded Michael about his weight. Mom always yells at me for eating so much, he thought sadly. I can't help it if I'm fat. And I wish Dad wouldn't always tell me to be on teams. I don't like baseball or soccer. Everyone knows I'm not good at sports. Dad always says, "You'll be fat all your life, if you don't play on a team!" Michael remembered.

Then he thought, I hate it when Ali tells on me. She always tells Mom when I have any cookies. She tells on everything I do. And I HATE it when she calls me fatty. "Mom, Michael-the-fatty is eating cookies in the back yard!" she says.

Dad doesn't give Ali a list of things to do while he's gone. But he says to me, "Come here, Michael. Let's see your list. Look at how much you didn't finish this week! Why didn't you get the garage cleaned out? You didn't rake the lawn, either. Can't you ever get your work done? You'll never amount to anything. When I was your age, I had to work hard."

But I can't do some of those things, thought Michael. Dad gets mad at Mom for not making me do everything on the list. Then she gets angry and they fight. It's all my fault. If I wasn't there, maybe they wouldn't fight so much.

Why does Dad always want everything to be perfect? Michael wondered. I remember once when he yelled at me for not putting his tools away. "Why can't you ever do anything right? Are you stupid? The hammer always goes right here and the screwdrivers are always

there. Can't you remember anything?"
Dad just thinks I'm supposed to know
all that stuff. I probably *am* dumb,
Michael thought sadly.

Mr. Mason came back in a rush. "Gee,
Michael, I'm sorry I was gone so long,"
he said. Michael was surprised to hear
Mr. Mason say that. It didn't seem like
a long time to him.

"While I was gone, did you think
about your family?" asked Mr. Mason.

Michael told him what he had thought
about his mother and sister. He told him
about the list and about the tools. "I
guess I'm just dumb," he said at the end.

"Michael," said Mr. Mason, "you are
not dumb." Then he said, "If you could
change things at home to be just like
you wanted, what would you change?"

Michael thought hard. What should he say? "Well, I guess I would like it if Dad didn't get so mad at me. I'd like to talk about things together instead of having him get angry. I'd like it if Mom wasn't always telling me to lose weight. And I'd like to be able to read books and watch TV without being yelled at to go play outside. I'd also like my parents not to fight. It always seems like my fault. And I don't want my bratty sister to bother me."

"You're talking about a lot of changes. I don't know if I can help with all of them, Michael. But, I want you to know that, when your parents fight, it is not your fault. That's between them. Maybe I can help with some of the other things, though. I'm going to see if your parents will come to school and talk to your teacher and me," said Mr. Mason.

"They'll probably be too busy to come here," said Michael.

"You let me worry about that. Now, what are we going to do about you fighting with the other boys?" said Mr. Mason.

"Maybe you could just tell them to leave me alone?" said Michael.

"What do you think you could do?" asked Mr. Mason.

"I don't know," said Michael. "Kids just pick on me all the time."

"I meet with six or seven kids after school on Tuesdays. We talk about how to get along better at school and at home. We also play some games and have a snack. Do you think you would like to join us? We call it the Friendship Club."

"Maybe I would," said Michael. "I suppose I'd have to ask Mom."

"Okay. You do that, and I'll call her to see when she and your dad can come here," said Mr. Mason. "And Michael, please try hard not to fight."

Michael went to his classroom. He was just in time for his reading group. He didn't feel so sad after talking to Mr. Mason.

When Michael came home from school that afternoon, his mom said, "I got a call from Mr. Mason at your school. Now what kind of trouble did you get into, Michael?"

"It wasn't my fault," said Michael. "Some boys were trying to steal my backpack. Mr. Mason saw it happen, and we talked about it."

Ali said, "They thought Michael had candy in his backpack. That's what they wanted."

"Are you sure you didn't start it?" his mom asked. "You always start fights with Ali."

"Really, I didn't, Mom," said Michael. He wanted to say that Ali started fights, too, but he didn't.

"Mr. Mason asked Dad and me to go to school for a talk with him and your teacher," she said. "I wish you wouldn't fight all the time. Then we wouldn't have to waste our time at school."

"Mr. Mason asked me to be in the Friendship Club on Tuesdays. Can I?" asked Michael.

"I don't see how, since your grades are so bad," Mom said. "Maybe later."

So, Michael had to wait. He remembered what Mr. Mason said about fighting. He didn't have any fights at school, and only one with Ali.

The next week Michael's teacher, Ms. Kline, Mr. Mason, and Michael's parents had their meeting. Mr. Boyd, Michael's father, didn't want to be there. He fought with Michael's mother. But Mrs. Boyd had talked him into going.

The adults discussed Michael's fighting at school. Ms. Kline said, "Some days Michael comes to school looking sad.

He seems worried at times, too. Then he doesn't do his work very well. I think he's a smart boy, but his work just doesn't show that."

Mr. Mason said, "I know Michael doesn't have friends at school. I'd like to help him with that."

After that, they talked about all kinds of things: the Friendship Club, and Ali,

and Michael's list of things to do. Mr.
Boyd said he thought that Michael had
things too easy. Mr. Mason talked a
little about what children usually were
able to do at Michael's age. Then, he
told Michael's parents how Michael
wished for changes at home.

Near the end of the meeting, Mr.
Mason said he thought Mr. and Mrs.

Boyd should see a counselor with Michael. "There seems to be a lot of things a counselor could help you work out together," he said.

"I'll think about that," said Mr. Boyd. "But Michael can go to the group on Tuesdays."

Michael found out a little about this meeting from his parents, and a little from Mr. Mason. He wondered what would happen.

Several weeks went by. Michael went to the Friendship Club and made friends with one of the boys. Michael's parents thought about counseling. Mr. Boyd learned that his company would pay for the family to see a kind of counselor called a psychologist. That is a person who helps people work out their problems. The Boyds decided to see this counselor.

For many months Michael's mother and father talked to the psychologist once a week. Sometimes Michael and Ali would go, too. The psychologist helped Michael talk about how his parents treated him and how that made him feel. His parents didn't know that the way they talked to Michael hurt him and made him sad. Little by little, his mom and dad learned better ways to talk to him.

They started to tell him when he did good work. They said nice things to him. When Michael didn't know how to do something for his dad, his dad showed him how. Michael's dad wasn't angry so much anymore. Michael's mom didn't talk about his weight as often. And no one in the family called him fatty. Not even Ali!

The psychologist helped everyone in the family. They learned to have fun together, and there weren't so many fights.

Not everything was perfect, but Michael liked his family better. He liked himself better, too. He even made some friends at school.

One day in the spring, Mr. Mason asked Michael into his office.

"Ms. Kline said you are doing much better in class, Michael," Mr. Mason said. "How are things going at home now?"

"Pretty good, Mr. Mason," said Michael. "We get along better now. My dad and I are even going on a fishing trip—just the two of us!"

"Hey, terrific. That's good news!" said Mr. Mason. "Are you still going to see the psychologist?"

"No. I kind of miss him. Talking to him was nice. At first my mom and dad didn't like him. They thought the whole thing was a waste of time."

"But that changed?" asked Mr. Mason.

"Yes, they kept going. Mom said she and Dad had to work out their problems. They are happier too, I think. At least they don't fight so much, and they're nicer to each other."

"That's good to hear," said Mr. Mason. Then he asked, "What are your plans for summer?"

"First, Dad is going to coach my

softball team," said Michael. "He said he would be the coach if I would play. So I'll try it. We've been practicing already. After softball is over, the whole family is going on a vacation for a week to the lake," said Michael.

"That sounds like fun. I'm glad things are better for you at home. You seem to feel better about yourself, too," he said.

"I do," said Michael.

Children and Emotional Abuse

In the story about Michael, his parents made him feel bad about himself. They always picked on him and made him feel stupid when he didn't do things right.

Many children feel that way at some times in their lives. They might feel unloved when their parents are angry or when their parents are too busy to talk or listen to them. That happens in all families. But when children always feel that way, it is called emotional abuse. Here are some things to know about emotional abuse.

- Emotional abuse is done mostly with words parents or other adults use when talking to children. Emotional abuse can be things like name-calling, telling a child that he or she is a bad person, or getting angry when a child isn't growing up as fast as a parent expects. Words can hurt. Words can cause children to feel terrible about themselves.

- Emotional abuse can make children feel that they are bad people. They might believe they are not loved, no good, or stupid. When children do not feel good about themselves, they don't get along with others. Often they have problems in school, like Michael did.

Usually, no one really knows what is wrong in the child's life.

- Most parents who act like Michael's parents at the beginning of the story don't know they are hurting their children. Some parents hurt their children more than Michael was hurt. And they don't always get help for the problem. Then the hurting can go on for a long time.

- Some parents go to a counselor or a psychologist like Michael's parents did. They learn that the way they talk to their children is hurting the children. Instead of using harmful words, they try to say good things to their children. They try to help their children feel better about themselves. This can take a long time. Many times, the children go with the parents to talk to the psychologist. They might talk with the psychologist alone. He or she can help the child feel better, too.

People to Talk With

Children need to feel loved and to feel good about themselves. There are many people who think you are special and can give you help and love. It is hard for children to ask for help when their parents hurt them with words. Here are some people who care about children and can help.

In the
family: Grandmothers or
grandfathers
Aunts or uncles
Older cousins

At school: Teachers
School social workers
School nurses

In the city
or town: Babysitters
Day care workers
Doctors or nurses
Neighbors

Words to Know

aide (AYD)—a person whose job is to help another person with his or her work

counselor (KOWN·seh·ler)—someone whose job is to help people work on personal, private problems or decide how to change something in their lives

emotional abuse (ee·MOH·shuhn·uhl uh·BYOOS)—when people say things that make someone believe they are stupid, clumsy, or bad when they are not

psychologist (sy·KAHL·uh·jist)—a person whose job is to work with people and help them understand why they think, feel, and act as they do, and who can help them solve personal, private problems

social worker (SOH·shuhl werk·er)—a person who works with people who have problems in the community where they live and work. A school social worker, like Mr. Mason, helps children who have problems in school

Note to Adults

In the story about Michael, we have attempted to describe how his parents' behavior toward Michael is damaging to his self-image. We've also attempted to show how sensitive school personnel can help a child with this problem. This is a very simplified version of a very complex problem; it is an attempt to educate children about emotional abuse and what might be done about it.

Emotional abuse usually is defined as verbal abuse or extreme demands for the child to perform beyond his or her developmental capability. It results in a negative self-image for the child and disturbed behavior. Another result is a lack of emotional growth and development.

Children have many emotional needs. Among them is a need for emotional closeness to the parents, expressed by affection and approval. Children also need consistency and security, which gives them their identity and a sense of belonging in the family.

Meeting the emotional needs of children, in addition to their physical needs, is not an easy task. It takes hard work, but it is work that is extremely important to the children's well-being. This is not to say that parents must be perfect to raise children. Most parents have at one time or another said things to their children that hurt them. This could occur when a child doesn't behave or when a parent feels frustrated. When hurting a child is an everyday occurrence, though, it becomes abusive and is destructive to the child. The child's behavior may then become worse, causing the parent to feel more frustration and hopelessness.

Counseling can help. So can parent groups and books. Some parents may recognize on their own that their manner of dealing with children is not good. They can have a better relationship with their children if they emphasize their positive behavior and don't dwell on negative behavior. In other words, they should tell the child when his or her behavior is good and show they are happy about it. And when the child misbehaves, the parent can tell the child that the behavior is what the parent dislikes, not the child. For example, if a child writes on a wall, the parent could say, "Writing on the wall is bad," rather than "You are a bad boy (or girl) for writing on the wall."

Parents who are emotionally abusive may need to learn what behavior can be expected of children at different ages. They also need to learn constructive ways to handle the child's negative behavior.

If you know of a child you suspect is emotionally abused, you might try to talk the parents into counseling. You might offer support and love for the child. You might encourage the child's participation in a group such as the Friendship Club to which Michael belonged.

It is not easy to identify emotional abuse because of differing values. Values vary among people, depending upon their background and culture. It is not easy to require parents to get help to stop emotional abuse, but an understanding adult can help the child. Simply praising or being positive about a child can often help that child feel better about himself or herself.

About the Authors

Deborah Anderson, Executive Vice President of Responses, Inc., has helped establish programs to aid both children and adults whose lives have been touched by abuse and neglect. Deborah developed and directed a sexual assault services program for the Hennepin County (Minnesota) Attorney's Office, and created the conceptual basis for Illusion Theater's internationally acclaimed production, "Touch," which presents information on abuse to children. Deborah has worked with students, teachers, and school administrators regarding child abuse and neglect, and has been nationally recognized for her work in the area of children as victims or witnesses in court.

Martha Finne, Director of the Children's Division of Responses, Inc., joined that organization after directing a survey of Minneapolis school children entitled, "Child Abuse and Neglect: From the Perspectives of the Child," the basis for these books. She has worked as a child abuse consultant, speaking to parent groups and elementary school staffs regarding child abuse and its prevention. Her background includes a degree in social psychology, counseling at the Bridge for Runaway Youth, and volunteer experience working with both public schools and social service agencies.

About Responses, Inc.

Responses to End Abuse of Children, Inc. is a
public nonprofit corporation which tries to
coordinate programs in all segments of the
community aimed at reducing family violence
and child abuse and neglect. The organization
works with both the private and public sectors to
develop the most constructive responses to these
problems.

In 1983 and 1984 Responses, Inc. conducted a
survey of Minneapolis school children to assess
the children's knowledge on various aspects of
child abuse and neglect. The responses to the
survey provided the framework for these Child
Abuse books.